# Chapter 1: The College Years

In a small, picturesque town, four inseparable high school best friends, Emily, Sarah, Lily, and Mia, began their journey into adulthood. They had it all in high school - beauty, popularity, and loving boyfriends. Life was a never-ending stream of parties and drama, where they were the queens of their high school kingdom. However, as they left for college, reality began to creep in.

The story begins in the fall of their freshman year. Each girl was attending a different college, miles apart from one another. Their worlds were expanding, but so were the challenges they faced. Emily was studying engineering at a prestigious university, and the academic rigor was a far cry from her high school days. Sarah found herself in a bustling city, majoring in business, and the fast-paced life was overwhelming. Lily chose to attend an art school in pursuit of her passion for painting, while Mia found herself at a liberal arts college, exploring the depths of her psychology major.

As the semesters passed, the high school mentality they clung to began to falter. The distance created a strain on their once-unbreakable friendship, and their boyfriends back home grew distant as well. The late-night phone calls turned into awkward silences and eventually fizzled out. Emily, who had always been the problem solver, was the first to realize that they couldn't live in the past forever. She started exploring new friendships and diving deep into her studies, slowly letting go of the drama that had surrounded her in high school. Her newfound focus brought success and a renewed sense of self.

Sarah, on the other hand, struggled with adapting to the fast-paced city life. She yearned for the simplicity of her high school days. But with determination, she began networking and honing her business skills. She joined clubs, met new people, and found her stride in her college environment. Lily, while facing the uncertainty of an art career, realized that her passion could be more than just a hobby. Her art began to evolve, reflecting the changes she was experiencing, and she found solace in her creativity. Mia, who had once analyzed the trivialities of high school relationships, delved into the complexities of human behavior in a more profound way. Her studies in psychology led her to understand herself and her friends better, and she used her knowledge to help them navigate the challenges they faced.

As the semesters passed, Emily, Sarah, Lily, and Mia grappled with the growing distance between them, both physically and emotionally.

**Emily's Academic Challenge:** The first few months at her university were incredibly challenging for Emily. The heavy workload, competitive environment, and the absence of her friends weighed on her. She missed the long nights they used to spend chatting and sharing their dreams. One evening, after receiving yet another tough assignment, she reached for her phone, the urge to call one of her friends almost irresistible. But instead, she took a deep breath and decided to tackle the problem head-on. She discovered study groups and academic resources, eventually emerging as one of the top students in her class. Emily realized that her strength didn't come from relying on the past but from adapting to her present circumstances.

**Sarah's City Adventures**: The city never slept, and neither did Sarah. The endless parties and distractions took a toll on her studies. She missed the serenity of her hometown and the close-knit bonds she had shared with her friends. One night, feeling lost in the chaos of the city, she decided to take a solitary walk and stumbled upon a small park. The stillness of the park, amidst the urban chaos, gave her a moment of clarity. Sarah understood that she needed to balance her newfound urban experiences with her studies. She created a study schedule and joined a local club with like-minded individuals, forging new connections and finding a sense of belonging.

**Lily's Artistic Exploration:** Lily's art school was a place of immense creativity, but it was also a place of self-doubt. She often compared herself to her exceptionally talented peers and struggled to find her unique style. One day, while gazing at a blank canvas, she had an epiphany. She realized that her art didn't have to conform to anyone else's standards. Her journey in college wasn't just about mastering techniques but also about finding her voice. She started experimenting with bold, unconventional styles that celebrated her individuality.

**Mia's Deep Dive into Psychology**: Mia's studies in psychology led her to understand her friends, and herself, on a deeper level. She recognized that their high school bonds had been built on shared experiences and emotions. As they ventured into different paths, those bonds evolved. Instead of viewing this as a loss, Mia saw it as an opportunity to explore the complexities of their changing relationships. She engaged in heartfelt conversations with her friends, discussing their aspirations, fears, and the transformation each of them was undergoing.

After Emily's realization that she needed to adapt to the challenges of her college's demanding engineering program, she embarked on a journey of personal growth and academic success. Emily's newfound determination to excel in her engineering studies led her to create a structured daily routine. She established a strict study schedule, joined study groups, and sought out academic resources. The library became her second home, and she poured her heart and soul into her coursework. As Emily became more involved in her academics, she also started making new friends who shared her passion for engineering. She discovered that college offered an opportunity to connect with like-minded individuals who could support and challenge her academically. Emily learned to strike a balance between her academic pursuits and her social life. While she still missed her high school friends, she realized that she couldn't spend all her time reminiscing about the past. She started participating in extracurricular activities related to her major and attending engineering club meetings.

There were moments when the coursework became overwhelming, and self-doubt crept in. But Emily had developed resilience. When she faced difficult assignments or exams, she didn't shy away from seeking help from professors and tutors. She began to see every challenge as an opportunity to learn and grow. As Emily's college journey progressed, she reconnected with her high school friends during breaks and holidays. They shared stories of their own challenges and growth, and she found that their experiences were not so different from her own. They supported each other, encouraging one another to pursue their dreams and to cherish their bond.

Emily's journey in college became a testament to her determination and adaptability. Her strength wasn't rooted solely in her intelligence, but also in her willingness to face challenges head-on, seek support when needed, and grow as an individual. Her ability to break free from the high school mentality and embrace her new life as a college student was a key part of her personal transformation. As the story unfolds, the other friends similarly embark on their own paths of growth and self-discovery, ultimately strengthening their bond as they navigate the challenges of adulthood together.

Sarah's college life in the bustling city was a stark departure from her quiet suburban hometown. The city was alive with a vibrant nightlife, and she couldn't help but get swept up in its fast-paced rhythm. Sarah's college was located in the heart of the city, known for its vibrant nightlife. The city never seemed to sleep, and neither did she in the beginning. She found herself attending parties almost every night, drawn into the exhilarating world of late-night festivities, live music, and trendy clubs.

It was as if the city was a non-stop celebration, and Sarah didn't want to miss a moment of it. The city had an air of freedom that was both exhilarating and dangerous. Sarah's initial excitement and curiosity led her down paths she had never considered in high school. She found herself attending events where drinking and smoking were commonplace. The peer pressure, the allure of trying new things, and the desire to fit in sometimes got the better of her. The haze of alcohol and the thrill of experimentation seemed like a rite of passage. Sarah shared an apartment with three roommates, each with their own unique personalities.

There was Mia, a fellow student from a different college in the city; James, an aspiring musician; and Karen, a law student. They often engaged in late-night conversations about their lives, dreams, and the challenges they faced. Sarah found that these discussions were more engaging and thought-provoking than any she had experienced before. Her roommates exposed her to different perspectives and ideologies, broadening her horizons in the midst of the city's chaos. As the parties and distractions became a regular part of Sarah's life, her academic responsibilities began to take a back seat. She missed classes, struggled to keep up with assignments, and saw her grades slip. She realized that her college journey was at risk of derailing, and her connection to her high school friends seemed distant.

Sarah's college experiences were a whirlwind of excitement, but they also presented her with a series of challenges. The city's allure, its endless parties, and the enticing distractions initially led her astray, taking a toll on her academic focus. Her roommates, while providing engaging conversations, also exposed her to new temptations. As the story progresses, Sarah's journey will involve a process of self-discovery and finding a balance between the vibrant city life and her academic responsibilities, ultimately leading her to a more fulfilling path of personal growth and adaptation.As Sarah continued to be drawn into the city's exciting nightlife, she found herself making choices she wouldn't have considered in high school. The allure of parties, drinking, and smoking was strong, and at times, she let herself get carried away.

## An Unplanned Transformation

Sarah's transition into this new city lifestyle was not intentional, but it gradually took her over. She began to make choices that surprised even herself, actions that she couldn't imagine taking back in high school. The once-responsible and caring friend was becoming someone unrecognizable to her old friends. As Sarah delved deeper into the party scene, her behavior began to affect those around her. She made remarks and engaged in actions that hurt her roommates, Mia, James, and Karen. Her words and actions left them perplexed, and her reputation began to shift from being known as a friendly and considerate person to someone they couldn't predict.

There were moments when Sarah found herself alone, pondering her behavior and choices. She saw the hurt in her roommates' eyes and realized that her actions were driving a wedge between them. She also noticed that her academic performance had suffered significantly. It was in these moments of reflection that she began to understand that her pursuit of a carefree lifestyle had led her down a destructive path. After a particularly wild night of partying, Sarah woke up with a pounding headache and a sense of guilt that she couldn't shake. She saw herself in the mirror and didn't like the person she had become. It was then that she decided to make a change, to seek help from her roommates, and to start mending the relationships she had damaged.

Lily's college journey was filled with moments of artistic exploration, but there were times when she couldn't help but compare herself to her peers, feeling either superior or inferior. Lily found herself surrounded by incredibly talented artists at her art school. There was one peer in particular, Sophie, whose work often received praise and attention. Lily couldn't help but compare her own art to Sophie's, feeling that Sophie's work was more refined and appreciated. At times, she thought her own art was superior in terms of uniqueness, but the comparisons were never-ending.

The constant comparisons took a toll on Lily's self-esteem. She began to doubt her abilities and the value of her art. Her once vibrant passion for painting was overshadowed by insecurity. She questioned whether she was truly meant to be an artist or if she should choose a more practical path. These feelings of inferiority were detrimental to her creative process and overall happiness.

Lily's self-doubt began to isolate her from her fellow artists. She withdrew from art discussions and critiquing sessions, fearing judgment and criticism. Her isolation only reinforced her sense of inadequacy and hindered her artistic growth. Lily's struggle with self-comparison had a direct impact on her creative process. Her art, once a channel for self-expression and exploration, began to feel forced and uninspired. The fear of not measuring up to her peers stifled her creativity, and she found herself producing art that no longer resonated with her true vision.

It was during a moment of crisis, when Lily hit a creative block, that she realized the consequences of her constant comparisons. She couldn't continue down this path of self-doubt and insecurity. She reached out to a professor and her close friends for guidance and support. They helped her see that art was a deeply personal journey, and that comparing herself to others was stifling her unique voice. Mia's deep dive into the field of psychology led to both positive and negative challenges as she delved into the complexities of human behavior.

Mia was intellectually stimulated by the challenging coursework in psychology. She was eager to explore the intricacies of the human mind and understand behavior from a scientific perspective. The academic challenges pushed her to expand her knowledge and critical thinking skills. Mia's studies enhanced her empathy and understanding of human emotions and behavior. She found herself becoming a better listener and a more compassionate friend. Her ability to analyze and interpret situations, including those in her personal life, improved significantly. Mia's newfound knowledge allowed her to engage in profound conversations with her friends. She could offer insights and support based on her studies, which strengthened her bonds with them. Her friends appreciated her ability to help them navigate personal challenges and conflicts.

Mia's deep understanding of psychology sometimes led to over-thinking. She would analyze her friends' behavior, dissecting their words and actions, which occasionally caused her to over-analyze situations and conversations. This could create unnecessary stress and anxiety. Mia struggled to separate her academic interests from her personal life.

She sometimes found it challenging to "switch off" her analytical mindset when interacting with her friends. This could lead to her appearing distant or too clinical in her approach to personal relationships. Mia's friends sometimes sought her out as if she were their personal therapist. While she was happy to help, this could be emotionally taxing, as she was dealing with her own challenges and self-discovery as well.

## Chapter 2: Breaking the High School Mentality

The turning point came when Emily, Sarah, Lily, and Mia decided to reunite during their junior year of college. They had all grown individually and realized that clinging to their high school mentality had held them back. They spent a memorable weekend together, reminiscing about the past but also acknowledging their growth. They decided that they needed to face reality and embrace their new lives while still cherishing the bonds they had.

Together, they supported each other as they graduated college, entered the workforce, and faced the myriad challenges of adult life. They learned that life beyond high school had so much more to offer, but it required them to be open to change, personal growth, and new experiences.

After the four friends had their transformative realizations in their respective fields of study during their junior year, they knew it was time to confront the high school mentality that had held them back. The summer break brought a welcome opportunity for Emily, Sarah, Lily, and Mia to come together once again. They chose to spend a weekend at Emily's family cabin, a place that held fond memories from their high school years. As they reunited, they shared stories of their college experiences and their individual growth journeys. The cabin became a symbol of their past but also a place to celebrate their futures.

During their weekend at the cabin, they candidly acknowledged how they had all changed since their high school days. Emily was no longer the quiet engineer, but a confident scholar. Sarah had found her place in the city and learned to balance her social life with her studies. Lily was no longer defined by self-comparisons but had embraced her unique artistic voice. Mia had become a pillar of support and wisdom in her friendships, thanks to her deep dive into psychology.

They also shared their aspirations and dreams for the future. Emily revealed her plans to intern at a prestigious engineering firm. Sarah talked about an upcoming entrepreneurship competition she wanted to enter. Lily expressed her desire to organize more art exhibits and turn her passion into a career. Mia discussed her intention to further her studies in psychology and work with underprivileged communities.

As they sat around a campfire one evening, they made a collective decision to confront the high school mentality that had lingered in their lives. They discussed how it had held them back and created drama in their friendships and relationships. They recognized that they couldn't continue living in the past and had to embrace the present and the future.

Throughout the weekend, they took the opportunity to rebuild their bonds and make new memories. They went hiking, shared stories, and even organized a mini art exhibit featuring Lily's work. They created a collective painting as a symbol of their commitment to facing the realities of adulthood together.

# Chapter 3: Navigating Adulthood

The reunion at Emily's family cabin marked a turning point for the four friends. They had collectively decided to confront the high school mentality that had held them back, and now they were determined to embrace the present and their evolving lives. The summer passed quickly, and the friends returned to their respective colleges for their senior year. They felt a renewed sense of purpose and a strong bond that transcended their high school days.

Emily excelled in her engineering studies and secured a coveted internship at a prestigious engineering firm. Her hard work and determination had paid off, and she was on her way to achieving her career goals. Sarah successfully entered an entrepreneurship competition, securing funding for her innovative business idea. Her time in the city had taught her resilience and adaptability, and she was excited about her entrepreneurial journey.

Lily continued to showcase her art through exhibitions and galleries. Her unique style and newfound confidence in her work were garnering attention and praise from the art community. Mia's deep dive into psychology led her to an internship with a renowned therapist. She was gaining valuable experience and was set to graduate with a strong understanding of human behavior.

As they approached graduation, they realized that their paths were diverging even further. Emily was considering job offers in different cities, while Sarah was preparing to launch her business. Lily was getting ready to make her mark in the art world, and Mia was pondering the next steps in her psychology career. The challenges of adulthood were becoming more apparent. They grappled with issues like financial independence, career choices, and the complexities of adult relationships. They sought advice from each other and leaned on the support of their close-knit friendship. Despite the physical distance that was growing between them, their bond remained unwavering. They held regular video calls, shared their triumphs and tribulations, and continued to be each other's pillars of strength.

As they approached their college graduation, they knew that their lives would take them in different directions, but their friendship had evolved and deepened. They had come a long way from the high school drama that once consumed their lives, and they were ready to face the realities of adulthood together.

As the friends entered their senior year of college, they were determined to face the challenges and embrace the opportunities that came with adulthood. Graduation was fast approaching, and Emily, Sarah, Lily, and Mia were excited yet apprehensive about what lay ahead. Their shared journey from high school to college had brought them closer together, and they cherished the newfound depth of their friendship. Emily's internship at the engineering firm had gone remarkably well. She was offered a full-time position upon graduation, but she also had offers from other cities. The choice between job opportunities and the prospect of moving away weighed heavily on her.

Sarah's business idea had gained significant traction, and she was preparing for its launch. The responsibilities of entrepreneurship were a constant challenge, but she had grown into a determined and adaptable leader. Lily's art was receiving increasing recognition, and she was being offered opportunities to showcase her work in prestigious galleries. The transition from student to professional artist was both exciting and daunting. Mia's internship with the therapist had provided valuable experience, but she was uncertain about her next steps in the field of psychology. The decision to pursue further education or enter the workforce presented a significant choice.

The friends shared their uncertainties and leaned on each other for support. Late-night video calls became a regular occurrence, where they discussed their goals, insecurities, and the complexities of adult life. The looming responsibilities of financial independence, career choices, and the intricacies of adult relationships were both exciting and challenging. They often found themselves offering advice to one another based on their individual journeys.

Graduation day arrived, and their college years came to an end. It was a bittersweet moment as they said their goodbyes, not knowing when they would reunite. Despite the physical distance that separated them, their friendship remained steadfast. They made a pact to continue supporting each other, even if it meant navigating their evolving lives from different cities.

# Chapter 4: The Evolution of Friendship

After graduation, Emily, Sarah, Lily, and Mia embarked on their individual paths, each moving to different cities and pursuing their dreams. Emily settled into her new job in a different city, embracing the opportunities and challenges of her engineering career. The distance from her friends was difficult, but they remained in touch through regular video calls and shared updates on their lives. Sarah's business venture took off, and her entrepreneurial journey was marked by both successes and setbacks. She faced the pressures of managing a growing startup, but her determination and adaptability were unwavering.

Lily found herself in a vibrant artistic community, where she continued to showcase her work. Her unique style gained recognition, and she embraced the freedom of expressing herself through art. She often hosted exhibitions, which brought her friends together to celebrate her success. Mia made the decision to pursue further education in psychology, enrolling in a prestigious graduate program in a different city. Her studies deepened her understanding of human behavior, and she felt a sense of purpose in her academic pursuits.

The friends continued to support each other, offering advice and encouragement, even from afar. They celebrated each other's achievements and provided a source of strength during challenging times. Despite their physical separation, they made an effort to reunite periodically. They planned vacations together, visited each other's cities, and made sure to create new memories to add to their collection. Adulthood brought its own complexities, including romantic relationships, work-life balance, and the occasional setback. The friends shared their experiences, offering a listening ear and a shoulder to lean on.

As the years passed, they recognized that their friendship had evolved but remained as strong as ever. Their shared history, mutual support, and unwavering bond continued to be a source of strength and comfort in their evolving lives. As the years went by, Emily, Sarah, Lily, and Mia continued to carve their paths in different cities and pursue their individual dreams. Their friendship remained a constant source of support and connection, even as their lives continued to evolve.

Emily's career in engineering was flourishing. She had been promoted several times and was now leading a team of engineers. Her hard work and determination had paid off, but the distance from her friends had taken its toll. She cherished their video calls and annual meet-ups, where they'd share stories and laughter, as it was the highlight of her year.

Sarah's business had its ups and downs, but her entrepreneurial spirit remained unbroken. She had faced financial challenges and competition, but her resilience saw her through. Her friends continued to be her biggest cheerleaders, celebrating her successes and offering encouragement during tough times.

Lily's art had become her livelihood. She had expanded her reach beyond local galleries and was now selling her work internationally. Her art continued to evolve, drawing inspiration from her life experiences and the different cities she had lived in. Her annual art exhibit brought her friends together from their respective cities, and it had become a cherished tradition. Mia's graduate studies in psychology had taken her on a journey of self-discovery. She was now a licensed therapist, and her research was gaining recognition in the field. She had found love in her new city and was navigating the complexities of a long-distance relationship. Her friends continued to be her confidants, offering advice and unwavering support.

Despite their busy lives and physical separation, they made an effort to reunite as often as they could. They traveled to each other's cities, explored new destinations, and created memorable experiences together. These reunions were a reminder of the unbreakable bond they shared. As they navigated adulthood, they faced new challenges, from managing long-distance relationships to the pressures of their careers. Through the highs and lows, they remained each other's steadfast allies, offering a listening ear, a shoulder to lean on, and advice grounded in their deep understanding of one another. The years passed, but their friendship remained constant. They had evolved individually, but the connection they shared was unwavering. Their collective history, mutual support, and unwavering bond continued to be a source of strength and comfort in their evolving lives.

# Chapter 5: Challenges and Triumphs

The friends' journey through adulthood continued to be a series of challenges and triumphs, with each of them facing unique situations and experiences.

Emily's career had taken her to new heights, but it came with increasing responsibilities and work-related stress. She grappled with the demands of her job and long hours. The support of her friends, who understood the pressures of adulthood, became an anchor for her. Sarah's startup had grown, attracting the attention of investors. Scaling the business presented new challenges, including managing a growing team and expanding into international markets. Her friends' business acumen and encouragement were invaluable. Lily's artistic journey had its share of highs and lows. While she continued to gain recognition for her work, the pressure of meeting expectations and staying true to her unique style weighed on her. The guidance and feedback from her friends, who appreciated the evolution of her art, were a source of inspiration.

Mia's career as a therapist was flourishing, but her long-distance relationship had its trials. The emotional toll of being apart from her partner tested her resilience. Her friends, who had supported her through ups and downs, were there to lend an understanding ear.

Adulthood also brought a series of life events, from engagements and weddings to moves and personal growth. The friends celebrated these milestones together and provided unwavering support, even from afar. Despite the physical distance that separated them, they remained committed to reuniting regularly. Their annual meet-ups had become a cherished tradition, a time to reflect on their journeys, create new memories, and strengthen their bond. They found solace in their friendship, a safe space where they could be their true selves, sharing both their successes and their vulnerabilities. Their unwavering support, understanding, and acceptance were a testament to the enduring nature of their bond.

Emily, Sarah, Lily, and Mia gathered for their annual reunion at a cozy cabin in the woods. As they sat around the fireplace, the crackling of the fire providing warmth and comfort, they began to share their recent experiences, challenges, and triumphs.

**Emily:** (with a weary smile) "Work has been crazy, guys. I got this huge project at the firm, and I've been pulling late nights almost every week. I miss you all so much. It's been tough."

**Sarah:** (nodding) "I feel you, Emily. Running the startup has its own set of challenges. We secured more funding, which is great, but managing the growing team and expanding internationally has been a roller coaster. Sometimes, I wonder if I'm cut out for this."

**Lily:** (reflecting) "I've had my share of ups and downs too. The art scene is both inspiring and overwhelming. I'm always striving to create something new, but the pressure to meet expectations sometimes feels suffocating."

**Mia:** (pausing) "My career in therapy has been fulfilling, but it comes with its own emotional baggage. The long-distance relationship has its tough moments. The support of my partner helps, but it's not always easy."

**Emily:** (reaching out) "We're here for you, Mia. No one understands the complexities of adult life like we do. That's the beauty of our friendship. We can lean on each other when things get tough."

**Sarah:** (encouragingly) "Absolutely. We're not just friends; we're each other's cheerleaders. Emily, remember that time you doubted your engineering skills? Look at where you are now. You're a rock star."

**Lily:** (with gratitude) "And Sarah, your entrepreneurship journey is inspiring. You've got this, no doubt. It's all part of the process."

**Mia:** (smiling) "And Lily, your art is evolving beautifully. Your unique style is what sets you apart. Keep following your passion."

## Chapter 6: Milestones and Reflections

As the years passed, the friends continued to navigate the complexities of adulthood, celebrating milestones, and reflecting on their individual journeys. They gathered for another annual reunion, this time at a beautiful lakeside cabin, ready to share their stories.

**Emily:** (raising a glass) "I can't believe it's been five years since we graduated from college. It feels like a lifetime ago. My work has been intense, but I was recently promoted to lead the engineering team. It's been a tough journey, but moments like these make it all worth it."

**Sarah:** (toasting) "Cheers to that, Emily! My startup is growing, and we just secured another round of funding. It's been a roller coaster, but it's incredibly rewarding. You guys have been my inspiration through it all."

**Lily:** (reflecting) "I've had a breakthrough year with my art. I hosted an exhibition in Paris, can you believe it? I never thought I'd make it this far. Your support and encouragement have been my driving force."

**Mia:** (grinning) "I finally moved in with my partner, and we're taking the next big step together. My therapy practice is thriving, and I've published my first research paper. The path to get here had its challenges, but you've been my constant source of strength."

**Emily:** (emotional) "I'm so proud of all of you. We've come a long way since high school. We've faced our own challenges, but we've always had each other's backs."

**Sarah:** (with gratitude) "This friendship is what has kept me going, no matter how tough it got. I'm incredibly grateful for each one of you."

**Lily:** (teary-eyed) "Our reunions have become the highlights of my year. I can't imagine going through life's ups and downs without you all by my side."

**Mia:** (nodding) "Our bond is unbreakable. We've celebrated milestones and faced challenges together, and there's no one else I'd want on this journey with me."

# Chapter 7: Life's Unpredictable Turns

As the friends gathered once again for their annual reunion, they had experienced life's unpredictable twists and turns, bringing them face to face with new challenges and lessons.

**Emily:** (gazing at the stars) "Life can be so unpredictable. This year, I faced a major setback at work. We had a project that didn't go as planned, and it was a tough pill to swallow."

**Sarah:** (with empathy) "I can relate. My startup had a rough patch too. We had to pivot our business strategy, and it was a scary decision to make. Your encouragement and insights helped me through it, even from miles away."

**Lily:** (nodding) "The art world isn't always rosy either. I had a gallery reject my work for a big show. It was disheartening, but it also made me rethink my approach. Your honest critiques have been invaluable."

**Mia:** (reflecting) "In my personal life, my partner and I faced some significant challenges this year. It tested our relationship, but we came out stronger. Your words of wisdom and encouragement made all the difference."

**Emily:** (grateful) "I've realized that it's during these tough times that I'm most grateful for our friendship. We've seen each other through highs and lows, and I wouldn't have it any other way."

**Sarah:** (with a smile) "You're absolutely right. Our bond is our constant, no matter what life throws at us. The support, the understanding, it's what keeps us going."

**Lily:** (teary-eyed) "Your unwavering support, even in the face of setbacks, is what makes our friendship so special. I couldn't have asked for better friends."

**Mia:** (with affection) "Life's unpredictability is what makes our journey together so fascinating. Through all the twists and turns, we've remained a constant source of strength for each other."

## Chapter 8: The Strength of Friendship

Over the years, the friends had faced and overcome countless challenges, celebrated numerous milestones, and navigated life's unpredictabilities. Their annual reunion took on a new dimension, emphasizing the remarkable strength of their friendship.
Each year, their reunion was a reminder of the unique bond they shared. The cabin by the lake had become a symbol of their enduring friendship, a place where they could be their true selves. Emily, Sarah, Lily, and Mia continued to excel in their respective fields. They encountered fresh challenges, but they had each other's unwavering support and understanding to lean on. Their friendships with each other's partners had also deepened over the years, further strengthening the web of connections that bound them together.

They recognized the power of their friendship in offering solace, guidance, and unwavering support through life's complexities. The annual reunions were a time for reflection, sharing stories, and being each other's confidants. As the years went by, their friendship continued to evolve, deepening in ways they had never imagined during their high school days. It was a testament to the strength of their bond that had been forged through the challenges and triumphs of adulthood. The reunion at the cabin was a time to celebrate not only their individual achievements but also the incredible strength of their friendship. They understood that, through it all, their bond remained their greatest source of strength and comfort.

Around the familiar fire at the lakeside cabin, the friends gathered for their annual reunion, appreciating the remarkable strength of their bond.

**Emily:** (smiling) "It's incredible how our friendship has grown. We've been through so much together. This cabin holds so many memories, and I'm grateful for all of you."

**Sarah:** (with warmth) "Our journeys have been filled with ups and downs, and our friendship has been the constant that's seen us through it all. I wouldn't be where I am without y'all."

**Lily:** (reflecting) "Our reunions have become the highlights of my year. We've supported each other, critiqued each other's work, and celebrated each other's milestones. It's been an incredible journey."

**Mia:** (with affection) "The depth of our friendship is something I cherish every day. We've seen each other at our best and our worst, and that's what makes our bond so special."

**Emily:** (nodding) "Through the years, we've grown not just as individuals but as friends. Our friendships with each other's partners are a testament to the strength of our connection."

**Sarah:** (grateful) "Our partners have become our friends too. It's a beautiful extension of our bond."

**Lily:** (teary-eyed) "We've faced the unknown together, and we've shared life's complexities with open hearts. I'm grateful for your support and the unwavering love of our friendship."

**Mia:** (reflecting) "Our friendship is a beacon of strength in a world filled with uncertainties. We're not just friends; we're each other's confidants."

## Chapter 9: Cherishing the Present

As the years continued to pass, the friends found themselves cherishing the present moment more than ever. In Chapter 9, they gathered for their annual reunion at the lakeside cabin, each one realizing the preciousness of the time they spent together.

They had faced countless challenges and celebrated numerous achievements. Their friendship had seen them through life's unpredictabilities and had grown deeper with each passing year. The annual reunions had become a cherished tradition, a time for reflection, shared stories, and deepening their bonds even further. Their shared history was a testament to the power of their connection, a connection that had been nurtured over years of unwavering support and understanding.

Each friend recognized that their bond was something to be cherished, a constant source of strength and solace as they continued to navigate the complexities of adulthood.
The cabin by the lake had become a symbol of their enduring friendship, a place where they could truly be themselves, share their experiences, and celebrate their individual and collective growth.  They understood that the present moment was a gift, and their friendship was the most precious thing they had. They vowed to continue nurturing their connection and supporting each other as they moved forward in their journeys.

As the friends gathered around the fire at the lakeside cabin for their annual reunion, they found themselves cherishing the present moment more than ever.

**Emily:** (with a contented smile) "There's something about this place that makes me appreciate the present even more. It's as if time stands still, and we can truly be ourselves."

**Sarah:** (reflecting) "Our journey has been marked by countless challenges and successes. These annual reunions have become a testament to our enduring friendship. I wouldn't trade them for anything."

**Lily:** (teary-eyed) "I've realized how precious our connection is. We've seen each other through the ups and downs of life, and there's nothing more beautiful than our friendship."

**Mia:** (with affection) "These moments with you are a reminder of the importance of cherishing the present. Our bond is the most precious thing we have."

**Emily:** (nodding) "I've come to understand that our friendship is a constant source of strength and solace. It's a treasure that has only grown deeper with time."

**Sarah:** (with a warm smile) "Our shared history is a testament to the power of our connection. We've weathered life's storms together, and we've emerged stronger each time."

**Lily:** (grateful) "The cabin by the lake is a symbol of our enduring friendship. This place, these moments, they're what I hold closest to my heart."

**Mia:** (reflecting) "We've grown together, seen each other through the complexities of adulthood, and our friendship has only deepened. I wouldn't trade it for anything in the world."

# Chapter 10: A Lifetime of Friendship

In the final chapter of their story, the friends found themselves at a different stage in life. Their annual reunion continued to be a cherished tradition, but it took on a new dimension as they realized that their friendship had truly withstood the test of time.

Emily, Sarah, Lily, and Mia had become parents, and their children played together, forging the next generation of their friendship. They had all accomplished incredible feats in their respective fields and personal lives, and their friendship remained a constant source of support and understanding.The lakeside cabin, which had witnessed their journey through adulthood, was now a place filled with the laughter and innocence of their children.Their shared history had deepened the bond of their friendship, and they recognized that they had truly grown up together.The annual reunions remained a time for celebration, reflection, and creating new memories, a testament to the enduring nature of their connection.

Each friend understood that their friendship was a lifelong gift, something that would continue to be a source of strength and comfort as they moved into the later stages of their lives. Their story was a testament to the power of friendship, a story of how four high school best friends had navigated the complexities of adulthood, celebrated milestones, faced challenges, and built a connection that truly lasted a lifetime.

**Emily:** (with a contented smile) "It's amazing to see our kids playing together. It feels like we've come full circle. The cabin is filled with laughter."

**Sarah:** (reflecting) "Our journey has brought us so far. We've achieved incredible things in our careers and personal lives, but our friendship remains the constant that grounds us."

**Lily:** (with a twinkle in her eye )"The cabin, which witnessed our journey through adulthood, now holds the innocence of our children. It's a beautiful transformation."

**Mia:** (with affection) "Our shared history has become a treasure. We've truly grown up together, and that's something to be cherished."

**Emily:** (nodding) "Our annual reunions are a time for celebration and reflection, a chance to create new memories with the people we love most."

**Sarah:** (with warmth) "Our friendship has withstood the test of time, and it continues to be a source of strength and solace."

**Lily:** (grateful) "Our story is a testament to the power of friendship, a lifelong gift that keeps on giving."

**Mia:** (reflecting) "Through every stage of life, our friendship remains our most cherished treasure. We've truly built a lifetime of connection."

# Chapter 11: A Lasting Legacy

The friends had reached a point in their lives where they looked back on the legacy they had created, not only as individuals but as a group of friends who had stood by each other through thick and thin.

They had each experienced personal and professional successes and had faced their fair share of challenges. Their annual reunions continued to be a source of joy and reflection, and they celebrated the enduring nature of their friendship. Emily, Sarah, Lily, and Mia had become grandparents, and their children and grandchildren shared the same bond of friendship that had been nurtured over the years. They had left a legacy of unwavering support, understanding, and love to their families, who saw the importance of strong friendships and the enduring power of connection.Their story was not just one of four individuals but a collective journey, a testament to the beauty of friendship and the impact it could have on the lives of those around them. As they looked back on their lives, they recognized that their friendship was their most lasting legacy, one that had touched not only their hearts but the hearts of those they loved.

**Emily:** (with a reflective smile) "Our journey has left behind a lasting legacy. It's not just the sum of our individual accomplishments but the testament of our friendship."

**Sarah:** (nodding) "Our annual reunions continue to be moments of joy and reflection. It's a celebration of the enduring strength of our friendship."

**Lily:** (with a twinkle in her eye) "The cabin now echoes with the laughter of our children and grandchildren. They've inherited not only our bond but also the understanding of what friendship truly means."

**Mia:** (with affection) "Our legacy is one of unwavering support and love. It's a gift we've passed on to our families, who have come to appreciate the importance of strong friendships and the enduring power of connection."

**Emily:** (reflecting) "As we look back on our lives, it's clear that our friendship is our most lasting legacy. It has touched not only our hearts but those of the people we love."

**Sarah:** (with warmth) "Our story is not just about us as individuals; it's a collective journey. It's a testament to the beauty of friendship and the impact it can have on the lives of those around us."

**Lily:** (grateful) "We've left a legacy that speaks to the enduring power of connection. Our friendship is a gift that keeps on giving."

**Mia:** (with contentment) "As we move forward in life, we do so with the knowledge that our legacy is not just in our achievements but in the hearts we've touched with our enduring bond."

# Chapter 14: Navigating a New World

As the children and grandchildren of Emily, Sarah, Lily, and Mia stepped into a world profoundly shaped by technology and social dynamics, they found themselves faced with the challenges of bullying in school and online, as well as the persistent issue of viewing others with disdain.

Olivia, Emily's granddaughter, was in high school and had experienced online bullying firsthand. She had also witnessed classmates treating others as if they were beneath them. Jacob, Sarah's son, was navigating the complexities of middle school, where he had witnessed the impact of cyberbullying and the exclusionary behavior of some students. Ella, Lily's granddaughter, was an artist, just like her grandmother, but she had faced criticism and unkind comments online that stung. Nathan, Mia's son, was studying psychology in college and was passionate about mental health advocacy. He had seen the consequences of bullying and the effects of feeling socially inferior.

These younger generations, inspired by the legacy of their parents and grandparents, embarked on their own journey to address these issues. They formed support groups, started online campaigns against cyberbullying, and advocated for kindness and empathy in their schools and communities.

**Olivia:** (addressing her grandmother, Emily) "Grandma, I've been dealing with online bullying, and it's been tough. People can be so cruel behind screens."

**Emily:** (with empathy) "I understand, Olivia. We faced our own challenges, but the digital world brings new complexities. It's important to be strong and stand up against it."

**Jacob:** (talking to his mother, Sarah) "Mom, some kids in my school are cyberbullying others. It's disheartening to see."

**Sarah:** (supportive) "Jacob, it's heartbreaking, but you can make a difference. Use your voice to spread kindness and stand up for those who are being targeted."

**Ella:** (sharing with her grandmother, Lily) "Grandma, I've received harsh comments on my art online. It's discouraging."

**Lily:** (encouraging) "Ella, remember that art is a form of self-expression. Don't let others discourage your passion. Stay true to yourself."

**Nathan:** **(discussing with his mother, Mia)** "Mom, the pressure and judgments in college can be overwhelming. I want to help others who are struggling."

**Mia:** **(proud)** "Nathan, you've chosen a noble path. Your empathy and understanding can make a real difference. Our legacy is one of supporting and uplifting others."

# Chapter 15: The Next Generation

As the children and grandchildren of Emily, Sarah, Lily, and Mia continued their journeys, it was time for their parents and grandparents to get to know them better.

Olivia, Emily's granddaughter, was a tech-savvy high school student. She excelled in science and was passionate about environmental issues. Olivia's inquisitive nature often led to engaging discussions about the future of our planet. Jacob, Sarah's son, was an aspiring musician with a talent for the guitar. He loved playing and composing music, often seeking inspiration from the natural world. Ella, Lily's granddaughter, was an accomplished artist like her grandmother. She had a unique style and was passionate about using art as a means of self-expression. Nathan, Mia's son, was deeply committed to the field of psychology. He was involved in various mental health initiatives on campus and was known for his compassionate and empathetic nature.

Their parents and grandparents, Emily, Sarah, Lily, and Mia, were eager to learn more about their interests, passions, and dreams. They spent time listening to their stories and sharing their own experiences, creating new bonds with the younger generation. As their parents and grandparents sought to get to know the children and grandchildren better, they delved deeper into their interests, passions, and dreams.

Olivia, Emily's granddaughter, was not only tech-savvy but also a passionate advocate for environmental causes. She often spent her weekends volunteering at a local nature conservation group, working tirelessly to make a positive impact on the environment. Jacob, Sarah's son, not only excelled at the guitar but had also formed a band with friends from school. His music was often inspired by the stories and experiences shared by his parents, creating a unique blend of melodies and lyrics.

Ella, Lily's granddaughter, was a prolific artist who was unafraid to tackle challenging themes in her work. Her grandmother's artistic influence could be seen, but she had developed her own distinctive style. Nathan, Mia's son, was deeply committed to his studies in psychology and had initiated a mental health support group on campus. His empathetic nature had been nurtured by his mother's guidance, and he was determined to make a positive impact on the lives of others.

As they shared stories, experiences, and passions, their bonds deepened, creating a sense of understanding and connection between the generations. It was a time of passing down not only the values and legacies of their friendship but also the unique talents and passions of the next generation.

As their parents and grandparents sought to get to know the children and grandchildren better, they engaged in heartfelt conversations about their interests, passions, and dreams.

**Emily:** (addressing Olivia) "I hear you're quite the environmental advocate, Olivia. Tell me more about your work."

**Olivia:** (enthusiastic) "Yes, Grandma! I'm part of a conservation group, and we're working on restoring the local wetlands. It's important to me to make a positive impact on our planet."

**Sarah:** (speaking to Jacob) "Your music is beautiful, Jacob. Have you been inspired by any particular experiences?"

**Jacob:** (thoughtful) "Mom, your stories about your travels have had a big influence on my songwriting. I love combining the beauty of nature with the emotions we feel."

**Lily:** (addressing Ella) "Your art is so unique, Ella. How do you come up with your ideas?"

**Ella:** (passionate) "Grandma, I draw inspiration from everything around me. But I also want to make art that addresses important social issues. It's a way for me to speak out."

**Mia:** (talking to Nathan) "You're doing some amazing work with that mental health group, Nathan. What drives you in this field?"

**Nathan:** (compassionate) "Mom, your passion for psychology has always inspired me. I want to help others who are struggling and ensure that mental health is a priority on our campus."

# Chapter 16: Celebrating Milestones

The family came together to celebrate a series of milestones, reflecting on the enduring strength of their bonds and the importance of support, love, and friendship.

Olivia graduated high school with honors, a testament to her hard work and commitment to environmental causes. Jacob's band had its first live performance, and his parents and grandparents were in the front row, cheering him on. Ella's art was showcased in a local gallery, a significant achievement that filled her with pride. Nathan's mental health support group had grown, and he was recognized with an award for his dedication to the cause.

The family gathered to celebrate these achievements, reminiscing about the journey that had led them to this point. The milestones were a reminder of the enduring legacy of friendship and support that had been passed down through the generations. As they raised a toast to the achievements of the younger members of the family, they recognized that their bonds had grown stronger over the years and would continue to do so in the future.

As the family gathered to celebrate a series of significant milestones, conversations flowed, filled with pride, joy, and reflections on their enduring bonds.

**Emily:** (raising her glass) "To Olivia, our passionate environmentalist! We're so proud of your high school graduation with honors. Your dedication is inspiring."

**Olivia:** (grateful) "Thank you, Grandma. I couldn't have done it without the support of our family, who instilled in me the importance of protecting our planet."

**Sarah:** (cheering) "And to Jacob, our rock star! Your first live performance was amazing. Your music is a testament to the power of self-expression."

**Jacob:** (blushing) "Thanks, Mom. Your stories about the beauty of nature always inspired me, and I wanted to capture that in my music."

**Lily:** (admiring) "Ella, your art showcased in a gallery is remarkable. Your unique style and the depth of your work leave me in awe."

**Ella:** (humbled) "Grandma, your artistic guidance has been invaluable. You've taught me that art can be a powerful medium for speaking out."

**Mia:** (with pride) "Nathan, your dedication to mental health advocacy has made a real impact on your campus. Your work is changing lives."

**Nathan:** (appreciative) "Mom, your passion for psychology and understanding people's emotions have always been my inspiration. It's a field where I can truly make a difference."

Their conversations were filled with love, pride, and appreciation for each other's accomplishments. The milestones were a testament to the enduring strength of their bonds and the legacy of friendship that continued to grow with each generation. They celebrated their achievements with a deep understanding of the importance of nurturing these bonds and supporting each other on their individual journeys.

## Passing Down the Traditions

The family continued to pass down the traditions, values, and legacies that had been central to their friendship and connection.

The annual reunion at the lakeside cabin remained a cherished tradition, a time for reflection, celebration, and strengthening their bonds. The younger generations were actively involved in organizing the event, ensuring that the traditions were passed on to the next generation. They spent their time hiking, sharing stories, and engaging in activities that had become a part of their family's history. The conversations were filled with laughter, shared memories, and discussions about the enduring importance of their friendship. It was also a time to honor and remember their parents and grandparents who had laid the foundation for their close-knit family.

Their conversations were filled with a deep sense of gratitude for the enduring friendship and support that had been the foundation of their family. The cabin held not only memories but a legacy of love and connection that they were determined to continue nurturing for generations to come.

## Chapter 18: A New Generation

In this chapter, the family embraced a new generation, as the children and grandchildren of Olivia, Jacob, Ella, and Nathan embarked on their own journeys.

The legacy of friendship, support, and nurturing strong connections continued to be at the heart of their family. The annual reunion at the lakeside cabin remained a tradition, passed down to the new generation with enthusiasm. The younger members of the family began to forge their own bonds, creating memories and traditions of their own. Conversations were filled with advice, stories, and the passing down of values that had sustained their family for generations. As they welcomed the newest members into their circle, they were filled with hope for the future and a sense of continuity that had marked their family's history.

As Olivia, Jacob, Ella, and Nathan's children and grandchildren continued to embark on their own journeys, there was a new addition to the family that added a unique twist to their story. Evelyn, Olivia's daughter, was a bright and enthusiastic teenager who shared her mother's passion for environmental causes. She was actively involved in her high school's ecology club and dreamed of a career as an environmental scientist. Lucas, Jacob's son, was a talented musician like his father, but he had a unique twist. Lucas was born blind and had an extraordinary ability to create beautiful melodies without ever having seen the world. Sophie, Ella's daughter, was an artist just like her mother and grandmother. Her art had a whimsical quality, and she had an uncanny ability to capture the essence of nature in her paintings.

Aiden, Nathan's son, had inherited his father's empathy and had a deep interest in psychology. However, Aiden was non-binary, and their journey of self-discovery and acceptance was a testament to the family's open-mindedness and support.

*The introduction of Aiden and their unique identity added a beautiful twist to the family's story, highlighting the importance of acceptance, love, and understanding. It was a reminder that their legacy of friendship and connection was rooted in embracing the uniqueness of each family member and supporting them in their individual journeys.*

# Chapter 19: A World of Sound and Music

In this chapter, the family delved into the life and experiences of Lucas, Jacob's son, who had been born blind and had found his unique path as a musician.

Lucas's world was one of sound and touch, and he had an extraordinary ability to connect with music on a profound level. He had learned to play multiple instruments by ear, from the guitar to the piano, creating melodies that resonated with the soul. Lucas had a remarkable gift for composing music that captured the beauty and emotions of the world around him, despite never having seen it. His journey had not been without challenges, but he had overcome them with determination and the unwavering support of his family. The family celebrated Lucas's music, recognizing that it was a testament to the power of passion, determination, and embracing one's unique abilities.

As the family delved into Lucas's life and his journey as a musician, they also explored his experiences of being blind in school. Lucas had attended a school for the visually impaired, which had provided a supportive environment and equipped him with valuable skills for navigating the world as a blind individual. He had faced challenges that sighted students couldn't fully understand, from using braille for reading and writing to learning to navigate with a cane.

Lucas had also encountered misconceptions and stereotypes about blindness, but he had embraced these moments as opportunities to educate others about his unique perspective. His love for music had blossomed during his school years, thanks to dedicated music instructors who had recognized his extraordinary talent. Through the challenges and triumphs of his school years, Lucas had developed resilience, a strong sense of self, and a deep connection to the world of music that was as vivid as any sighted person's view of the world.

The family celebrated Lucas's strength and determination, acknowledging the unique path he had walked and the beautiful music he had created along the way. His story was a testament to the power of embracing one's uniqueness and pursuing one's dreams with unwavering passion.

# Chapter 20: Embracing Uniqueness

In this chapter, the family explored the life and experiences of Aiden, Nathan's child, who identified as non-binary, and how this uniqueness had shaped their life and influenced family traditions.

Aiden was a kind, compassionate, and open-minded individual who had always felt that their identity didn't conform to traditional gender norms. Their journey of self-discovery had involved challenges and triumphs, but it had been marked by unwavering support from their family. Aiden had been an advocate for gender diversity in their school, educating their peers about what it meant to be non-binary and promoting acceptance and understanding.

Their presence had gradually led to changes in family traditions, such as introducing gender-neutral language and promoting a more inclusive approach to gatherings and celebrations. The family had embraced these changes with open hearts, recognizing that love, support, and acceptance were the cornerstones of their enduring friendship and bond.

As the family explored Aiden's journey and their unique identity as a non-binary individual, they delved deeper into Aiden's life during school and the type of person they had become. Aiden had been a beacon of acceptance and understanding in their school, where they had been actively involved in the LGBTQ+ community. Their friends and classmates admired Aiden for their compassion, empathy, and advocacy for gender diversity. Aiden's school experience had involved moments of educating others about what it meant to be non-binary and challenging stereotypes and misconceptions about gender. Despite the challenges, they had found their own community of friends who accepted them for who they were, and their unwavering determination had earned them respect and admiration. Their unique journey had inspired openness within their family, leading to a shift in family traditions towards greater inclusivity and understanding.

**Aiden's Friend 1:** "Aiden, I've always admired your confidence and knowledge about LGBTQ+ issues. Can you explain to us what it means to be non-binary?"

**Aiden:** "Of course! Being non-binary means not identifying as exclusively male or female. It's about a gender identity that doesn't fit within the traditional binary concept. It's important to understand that gender is a spectrum, and non-binary individuals exist along that spectrum."

**Aiden's Friend 2:** "That makes sense, but why is it important to use gender-neutral language and pronouns?"

**Aiden:** "Great question! Using gender-neutral language and pronouns like 'they/them' is crucial because it respects and validates a person's identity. It's all about making people feel seen and accepted for who they are. It may seem like a small change, but it has a big impact on someone's well-being."

**Aiden's Friend 3:** "And what about the LGBTQ+ acronym? I've heard people add more letters to it. What do they all mean?"

**Aiden:** "LGBTQ+ is an acronym that stands for Lesbian, Gay, Bisexual, Trans gender, Queer (or Questioning), and the plus sign is used to be inclusive of other identities like pan-sexual, asexual, and more. It's a way of acknowledging and celebrating the diversity of gender and sexual identities within our community."

**Aiden's Friend 4:** "It's so great that you're knowledgeable about this stuff, Aiden. How can we be better allies and support our LGBTQ+ friends?"

**Aiden:** "Being an ally is all about listening, learning, and standing up for your friends when they face discrimination or prejudice. It's also about being open to having conversations, like the one we're having now, to promote understanding and acceptance. Allies play a crucial role in creating a more inclusive and diverse world."

*Their conversations were filled with openness and a genuine desire to learn and understand, reflecting the importance of educating others about LGBTQ+ issues and promoting acceptance within their school community. Aiden's role as an advocate and educator was evident, and their friends appreciated the opportunity to gain insight into the experiences of non-binary individuals and the broader LGBTQ+ community.*

**Aiden's Friend 5:** (with a somber tone) "Aiden, I have something to talk to you about. I've been struggling with my identity lately. I think I might be bisexual, but I don't feel fully accepted in the regular community."

**Aiden:** (supportive) "I'm really glad you reached out to me. You're not alone in feeling this way. Many people go through a period of self-discovery, and it can be challenging. But remember, you're valid just as you are, and there's a loving and accepting community that's here for you."

**Aiden's Friend 5:** (teary-eyed) "It's just that I'm afraid to tell my friends and family. What if they don't understand or accept me for who I am?"

**Aiden:** "It's normal to feel scared, but it's important to prioritize your own well-being and authenticity. Take your time with sharing this part of yourself, and choose people you trust and feel safe with. When you're ready, you can also find support from LGBTQ+ organizations and allies."

**Aiden's Friend 5:** (calming down) "Thanks, Aiden. I needed to hear that. It just feels good to talk to someone who understands."

**Aiden:** "I'm here for you, and you have a whole community that will support and accept you for who you are. You're never alone on this journey."

*This heartfelt conversation highlighted the importance of having a supportive friend like Aiden, who provided comfort and guidance to those struggling with their identities and acceptance. It emphasized the significance of finding understanding and loving communities within the LGBTQ+ spectrum and beyond.*

**Aiden's Peer:** (confused) "Hey, Aiden, I've got something on my mind, and I don't know who else to talk to. I'm in a relationship with my girlfriend, and I love her, but I've also realized that I have feelings for men. I'm not sure how to tell her."

**Aiden:** (empathetic) "I'm glad you feel comfortable talking to me about this. It's essential to be honest with your partner, but it can be really challenging. Start by reflecting on your feelings and understanding them better. When you're ready, have an open and honest conversation with your girlfriend. It's important to communicate your feelings, but also be prepared for her reaction, whatever it may be."

**Aiden's Peer:** (worried) "I just don't want to hurt her. She means a lot to me, and I don't want to lose her because of this."

**Aiden:** "I understand your concern. It's important to emphasize that your feelings for her are genuine. You're still the same person she fell in love with. But it's also crucial to be true to yourself. Honesty can lead to a deeper understanding, and you both can decide together how to move forward."

**Aiden's Peer:** (grateful) "Thanks, Aiden. Your advice means a lot. I'll have that conversation with her when I feel ready."

**Aiden:** "I'm here to support you through this. Remember, it's a challenging journey, but being true to yourself is a step toward personal growth and self-acceptance."

*This conversation addressed the complexities of being in a relationship while realizing one's true sexual orientation. Aiden's guidance emphasized the importance of honesty and open communication, even though it might be a challenging and emotional process. It also highlighted the value of being true to oneself and pursuing personal growth and self-acceptance.*

**Aiden's Peer:** (approaching Aiden) "Hey, Aiden, I've got a bit of a personal dilemma, and I thought you might have some insights. I identify as gay, and I've met this guy who I find incredibly attractive. But here's the thing: he's not part of the LGBTQ+ community. I'm not sure if I should ask him out or if I should just respect his boundaries."

**Aiden:** (thoughtful) "I appreciate you coming to me with this, and it's great that you're considering both your feelings and his boundaries. First and foremost, it's important to remember that attraction isn't limited by gender or sexuality. People can form connections regardless of their labels. If you genuinely want to get to know him better, it's okay to express your interest. Just be open and respectful about your own identity and his boundaries. Communication is key."

**Aiden's Peer:** (hesitant) "I'm just worried that he might not be comfortable with it or that he might feel pressured."

**Aiden:** "It's a valid concern. You can approach this conversation with a friendly and casual tone, without any pressure. Let him know that you appreciate his boundaries, but you're interested in getting to know him better. If he's not comfortable with the idea, respect his decision. Ultimately, it's about building connections based on mutual understanding and consent."

**Aiden's Peer:** (grateful) "Thanks, Aiden. I needed that perspective. I'll have that conversation with him and make sure it's respectful and understanding."

**Aiden:** "You're welcome, and I'm here to support you through this. It's all about being genuine and respectful in your approach. I wish you the best of luck."

*This conversation emphasized the importance of respectful and open communication when pursuing a potential romantic interest, particularly when there might be differences in identity and boundaries. Aiden's advice encouraged understanding and consent as the foundation for building connections.*

## Chapter 21: New Beginnings

In this chapter, the family celebrated new beginnings and the continued growth and evolution of their bonds. The annual reunion at the lakeside cabin remained a cherished tradition, a testament to their enduring friendship. The family had expanded with the addition of new members, and the cabin was filled with the laughter and joy of children and grandchildren. As the family continued to embrace diversity and individuality, their gatherings had become even more inclusive, with gender-neutral language and open discussions about love, identity, and acceptance. The family recognized that change was a natural part of life, and their bonds had only grown stronger with each new beginning. It was a reminder that love, support, and acceptance were the cornerstones of their enduring friendship, which continued to evolve and thrive with time.

**Olivia:** (with a smile) "Look at our family. It's growing so beautifully, generation after generation."

**Jacob:** "I'm so proud of the traditions we've passed down, like this annual reunion. It's a testament to our enduring bond."

**Ella:** "And the openness and acceptance we've embraced, allowing everyone to be their authentic selves. It's been a wonderful evolution."

**Nathan:** "It's incredible to see how our family has become even more inclusive, and the love we share continues to grow."

**Aiden:** (reflecting) "I'm grateful for our family's support and for all the conversations we've had that promote understanding and acceptance."

**Lucas:** "I've found my place within our family, just as I've found my place in the world of music. It's all about embracing what makes us unique."

**Evelyn:** "I've learned so much about the environment and how we can make a difference. It's inspiring to be part of this family."

**Sophie:** "Our art, music, and advocacy have shaped our family's identity, and it's a beautiful legacy."

**Aiden's Friend 5:** "This family's acceptance has meant so much to me. I'm grateful for your support as I explore my identity."

**Aiden's Peer:** "Aiden, I had that conversation with him. He was understanding and respectful. It feels like a new beginning for both of us."

*The conversations were filled with gratitude, reflection, and a sense of new beginnings. They celebrated the legacy of love, acceptance, and the enduring strength of their bonds as they continued to evolve and grow with each new generation.*

# Chapter 22: A Legacy of Love

In this final chapter, the family came full circle, reflecting on the extraordinary journey they had taken together and the legacy they had built. The annual reunion at the lakeside cabin remained a constant in their lives, a symbol of their enduring friendship and the legacy they had created. The cabin had seen generations come and go, each leaving their mark on the traditions and memories shared within its walls. They continued to pass down the values of empathy, support, and the importance of strong connections to their children and grandchildren.

Their story was one of a lifetime of friendship, of navigating the challenges and joys of life together, and of passing down the traditions that had bound them together. As they gathered one more time at the cabin, they were filled with gratitude for the enduring strength of their bonds and the legacy of love, support, and friendship they had built.

Chapter 23: A Legacy of Love

**Olivia:** (looking around the cabin) "This place holds so many memories. It's a testament to our enduring friendship."

**Jacob:** "Our children and grandchildren have embraced the traditions we passed down. It warms my heart to see that love and acceptance continue."

**Ella:** "The openness and understanding we've fostered have made our family even stronger. It's been a beautiful journey."

**Nathan:** "I'm proud of the way our family has evolved, embracing everyone's uniqueness and continuing to love and support one another."

**Aiden:** (reflecting) "I've seen our family's growth and acceptance firsthand, and it's been a beautiful journey. I'm grateful for the conversations we've had."

**Lucas:** "The music that fills this cabin is a testament to the power of passion and the beauty of individuality."

**Evelyn:** "Our commitment to environmental causes is something we've passed down, and it makes me proud to be part of this family."

**Sophie:** "Our art continues to be a reflection of our unique identities, and it's become a cherished part of our family's story."

**Aiden's Friend 5:** "Your support and understanding have meant so much to me, Aiden. I feel truly accepted within this family."

**Aiden's Peer:** "I talked to him, Aiden. It was a heartfelt conversation, and it feels like a new beginning for both of us."

---

*The conversations were filled with gratitude, reflection, and a sense of new beginnings. The legacy of love, acceptance, and the enduring strength of their bonds were celebrated as they continued to evolve and grow with each new generation.*

*And so, the tale of four high school best friends, their children, and their grandchildren, came to an end, leaving behind a legacy of love, acceptance, and the enduring strength of friendship. Their story would continue to inspire future generations, showing that no matter the challenges, love and acceptance would always be at the heart of their remarkable journey.*

*"Love is patient, love is kind. It does not envy, it does not boast, it is not proud." - 1 CORINTHIANS 13:4*

*"It does not dishonor others, it is not self-seeking, it is not easily angered, it keeps no record of wrongs." 1 CORINTHIANS 13:5*

*"Love does not delight in evil but rejoice with the truth." - 1 CORINTHIANS 13:6*

*"It always protect, always trust, always hopes, always perseveres." - 1 CORINTHIANS 13:7 "*

Milton Keynes UK
Ingram Content Group UK Ltd.
UKHW020636130724
445563UK00006B/35